The big plane

Story by Annette Smith
Illustrations by Pat Reynolds

Ben and Mom

looked for the big plane.

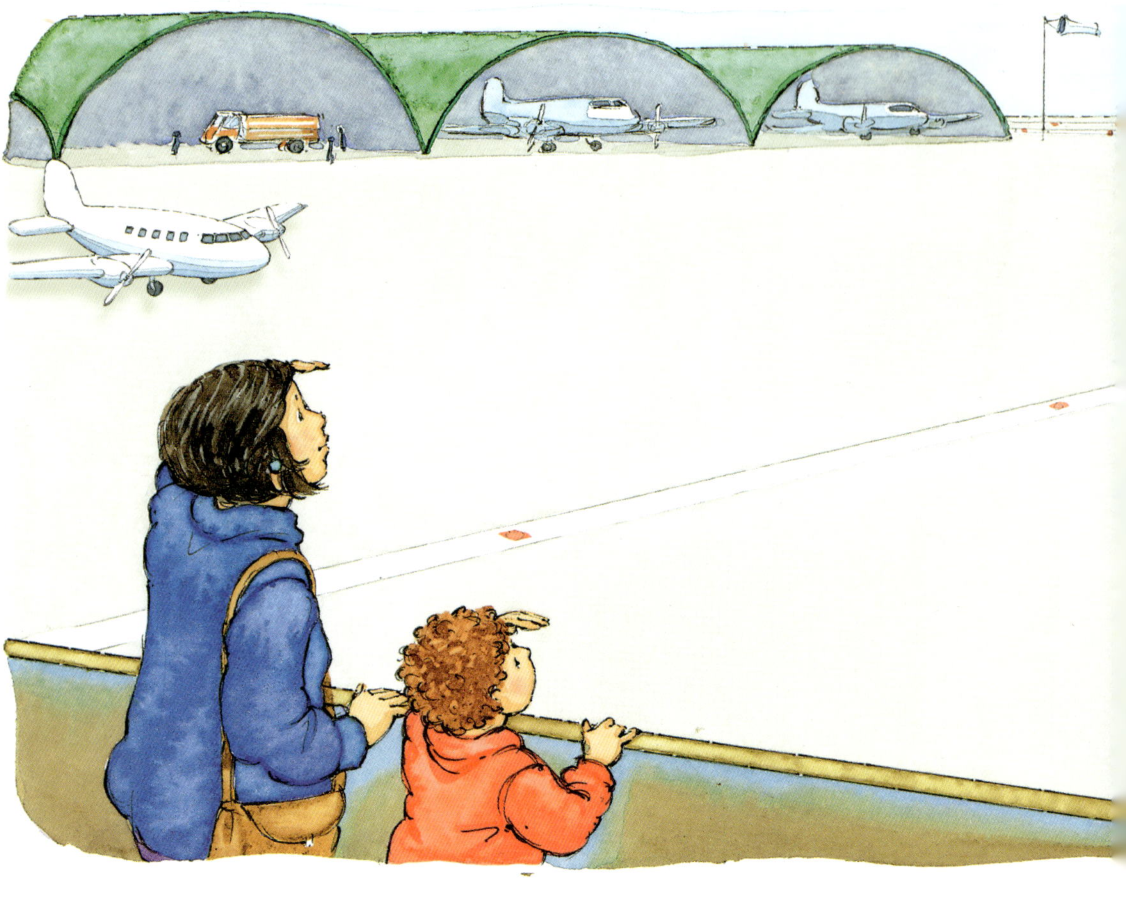

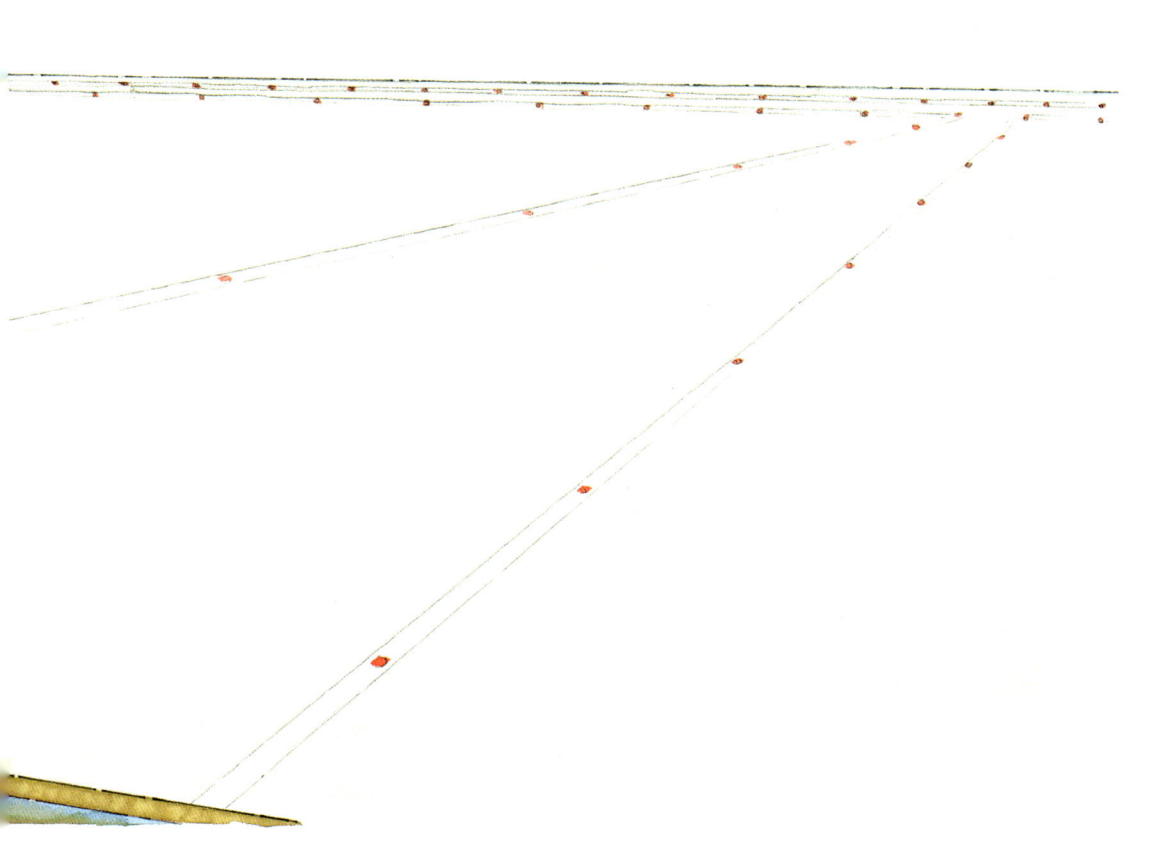

"Here comes the big plane,"

said Ben.

"Dad is on the plane."

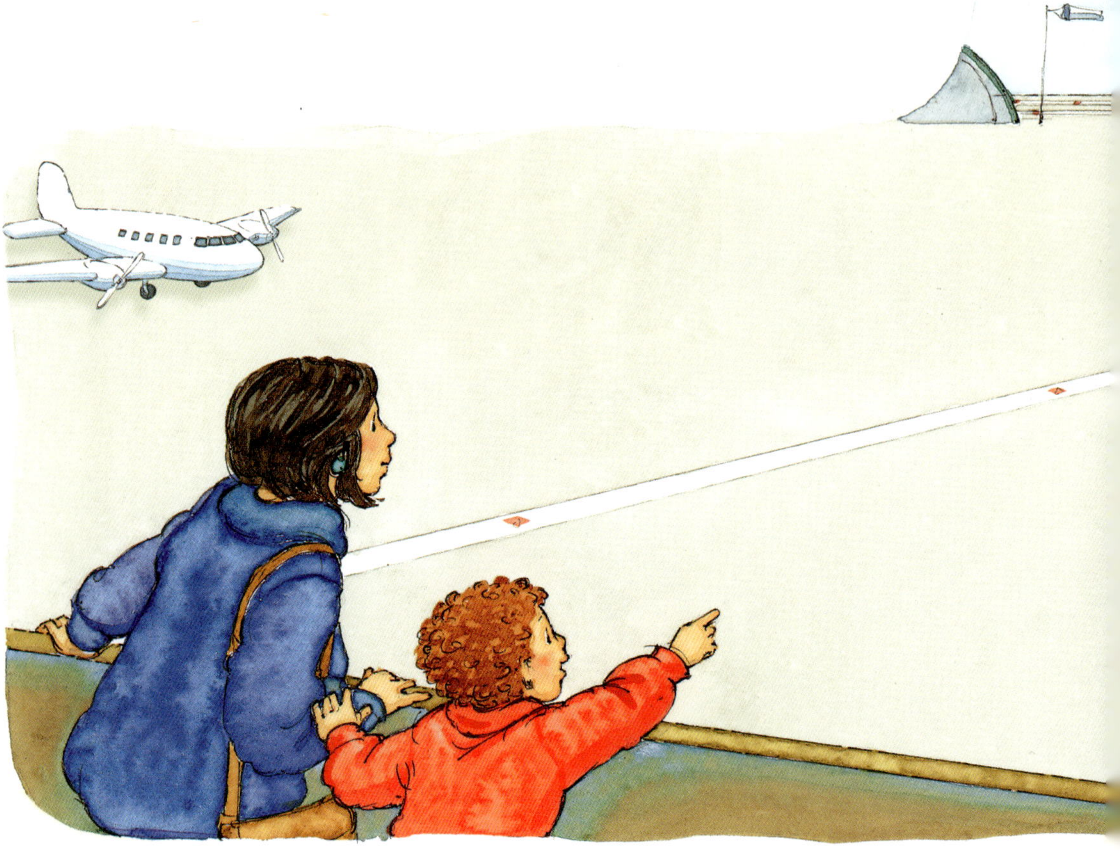

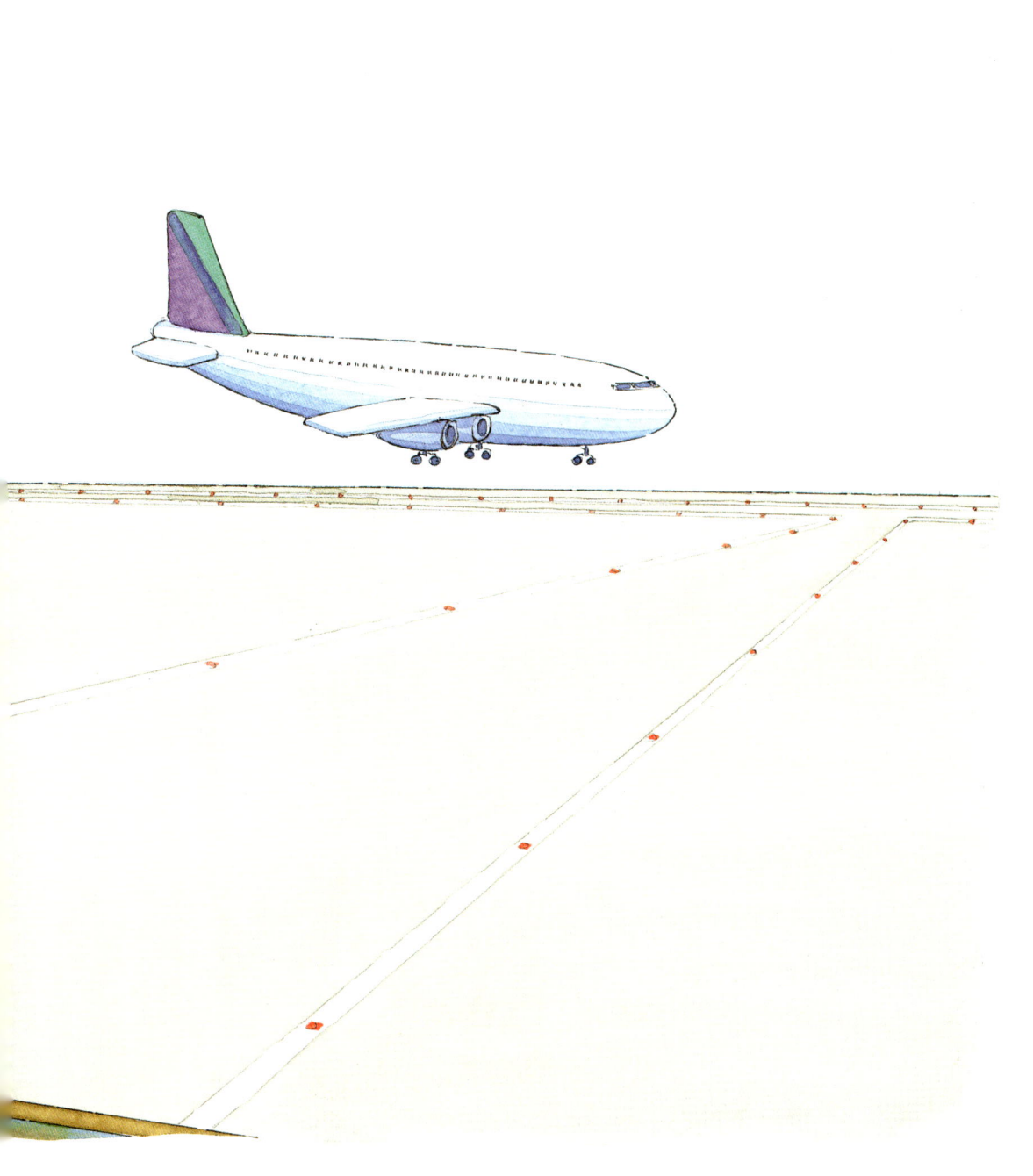

"Look, Mom!" said Ben.

"The big plane is here."

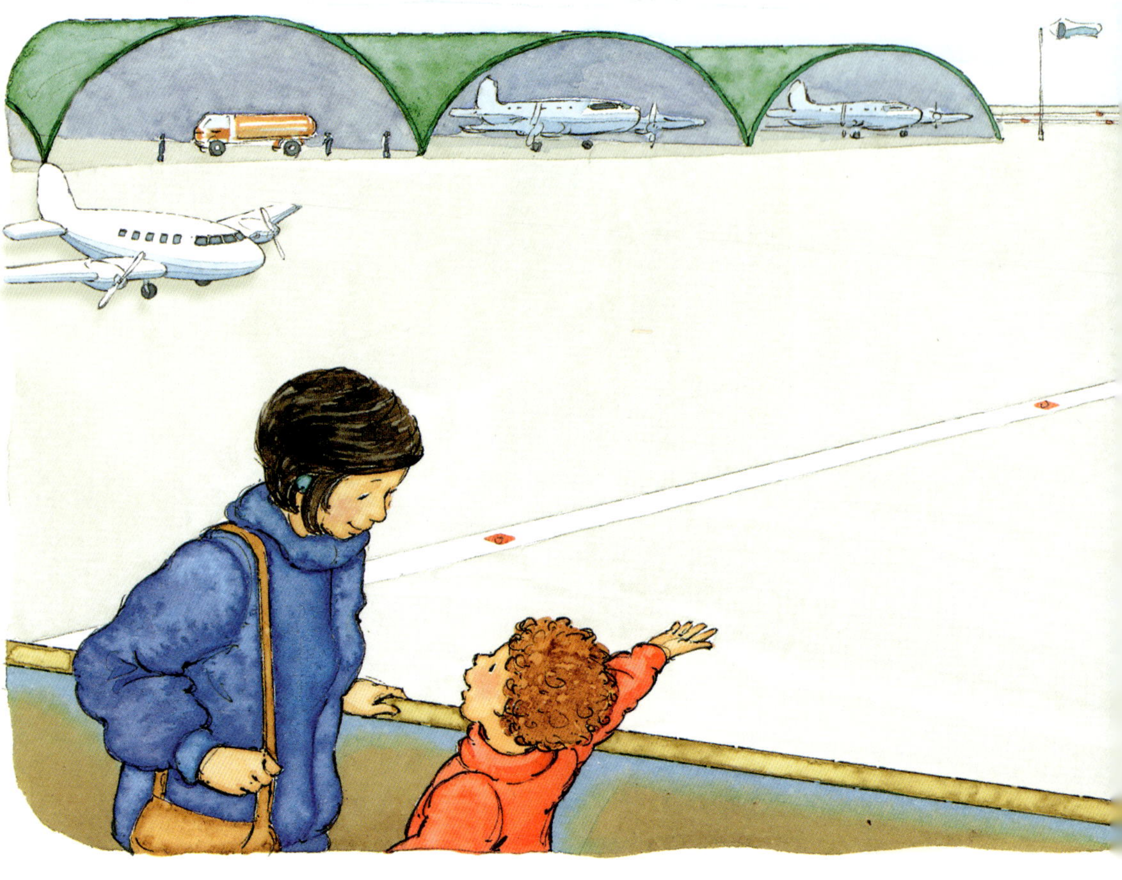

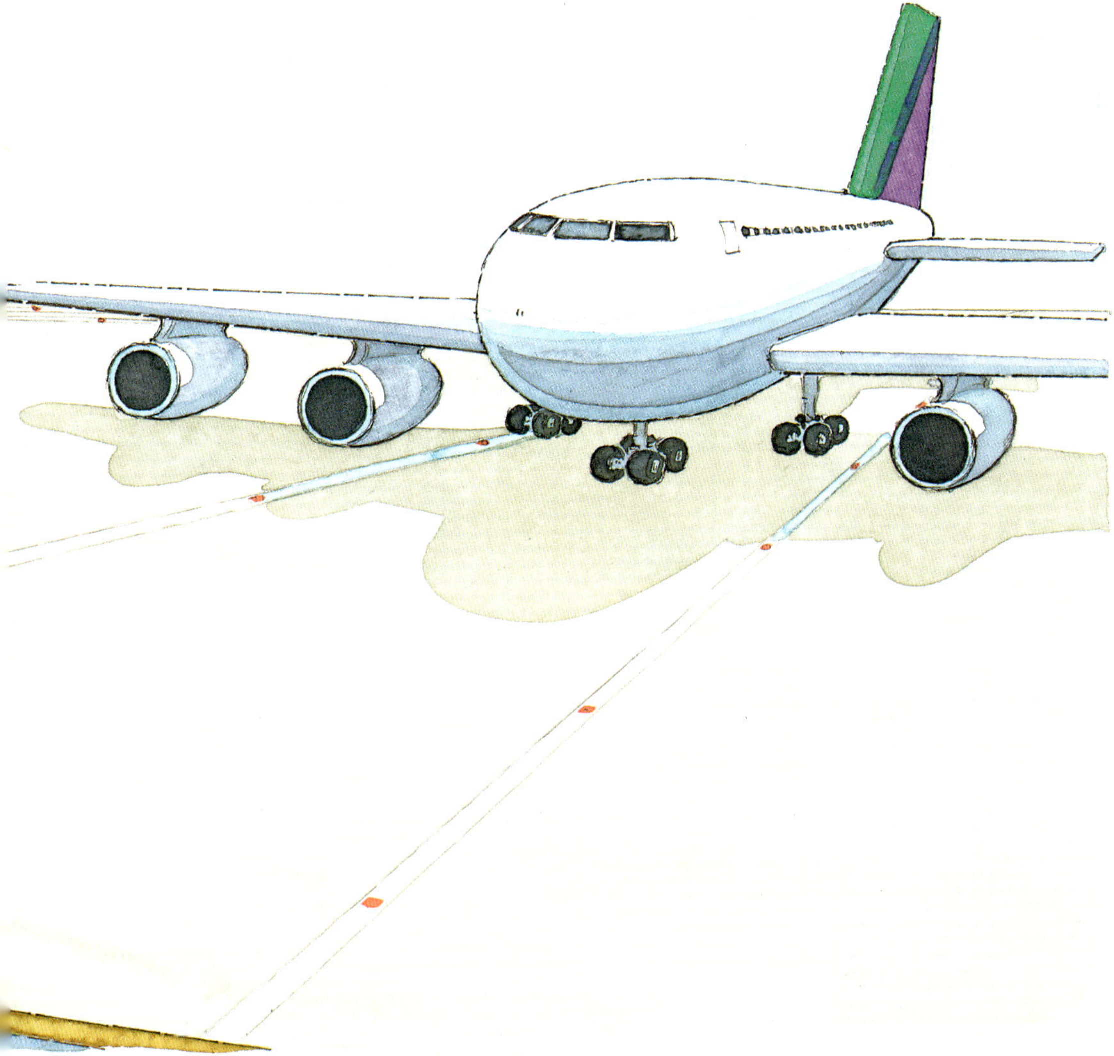

Mom and Ben looked for Dad.

"I cannot see Dad,"

said Ben.

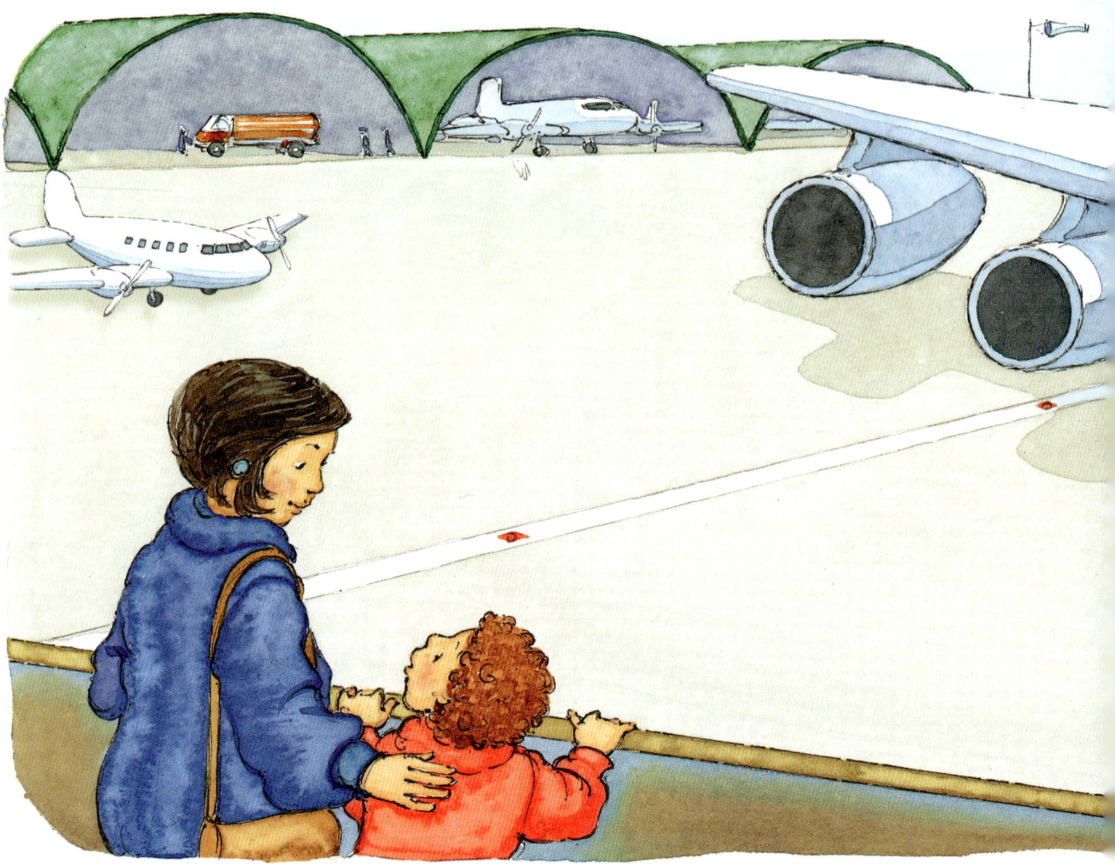

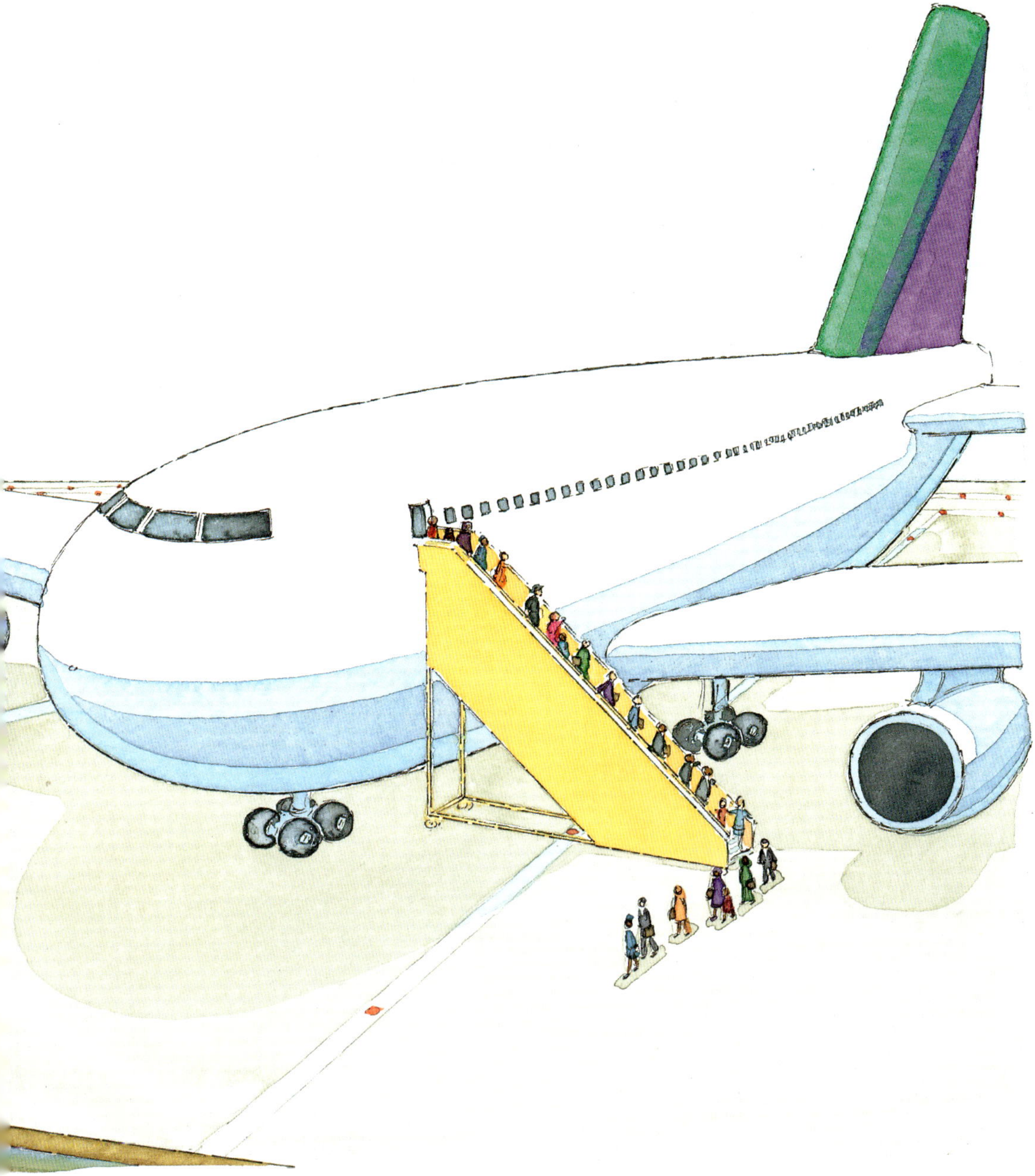

Mom and Ben

looked and looked for Dad.

Ben said to Mom,

“Can you see Dad?”

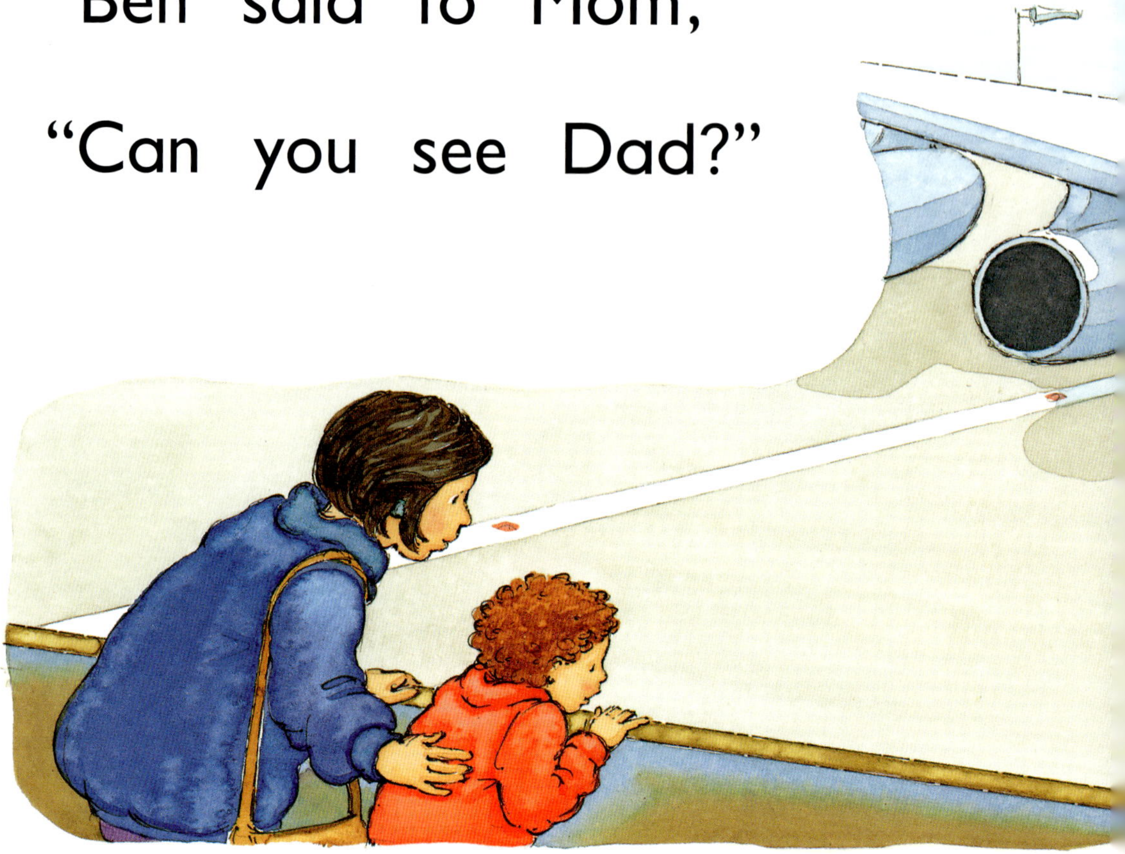

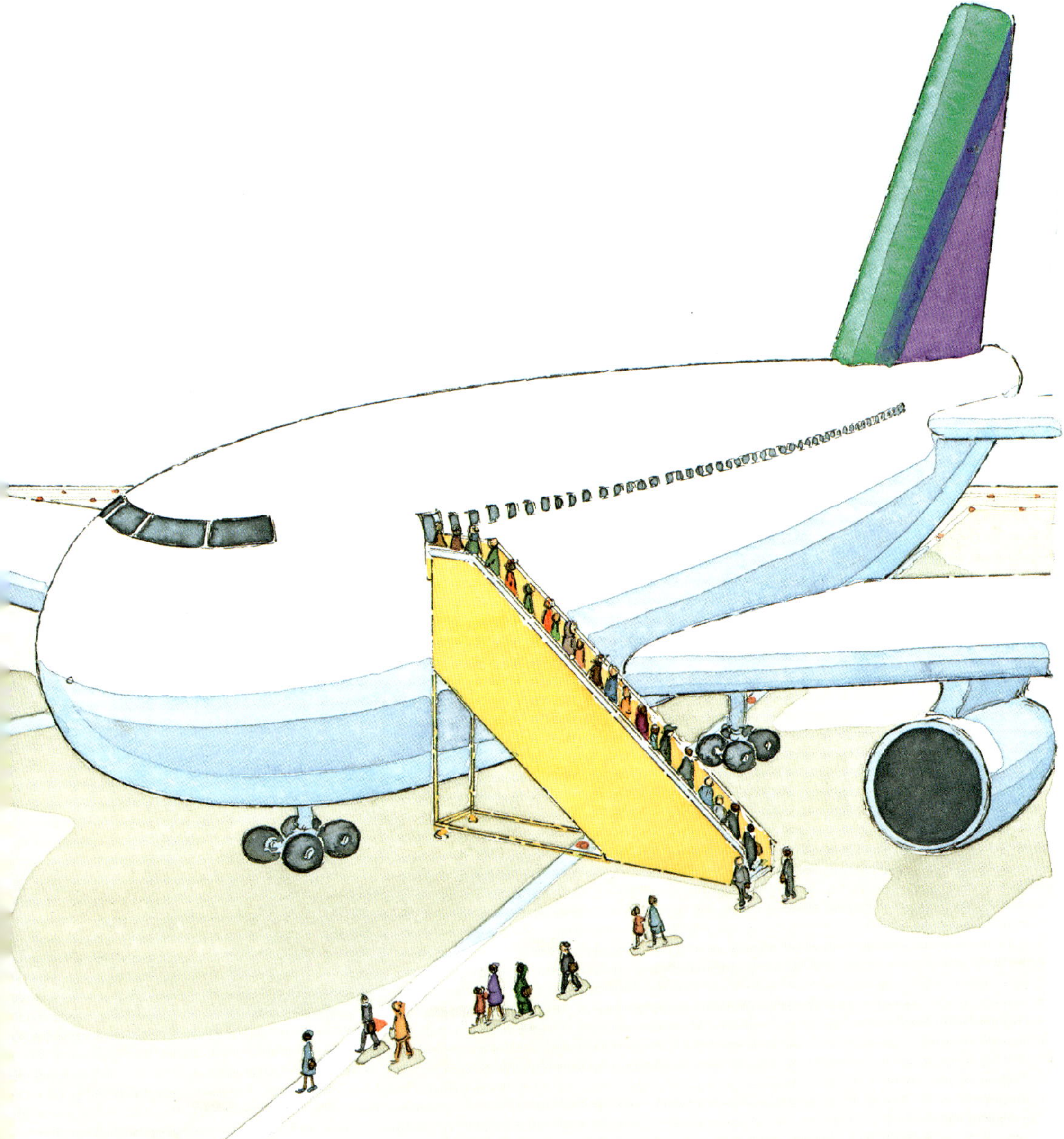

"No," said Mom.

"I cannot see Dad."

"Dad is **not** on the plane," said Ben.

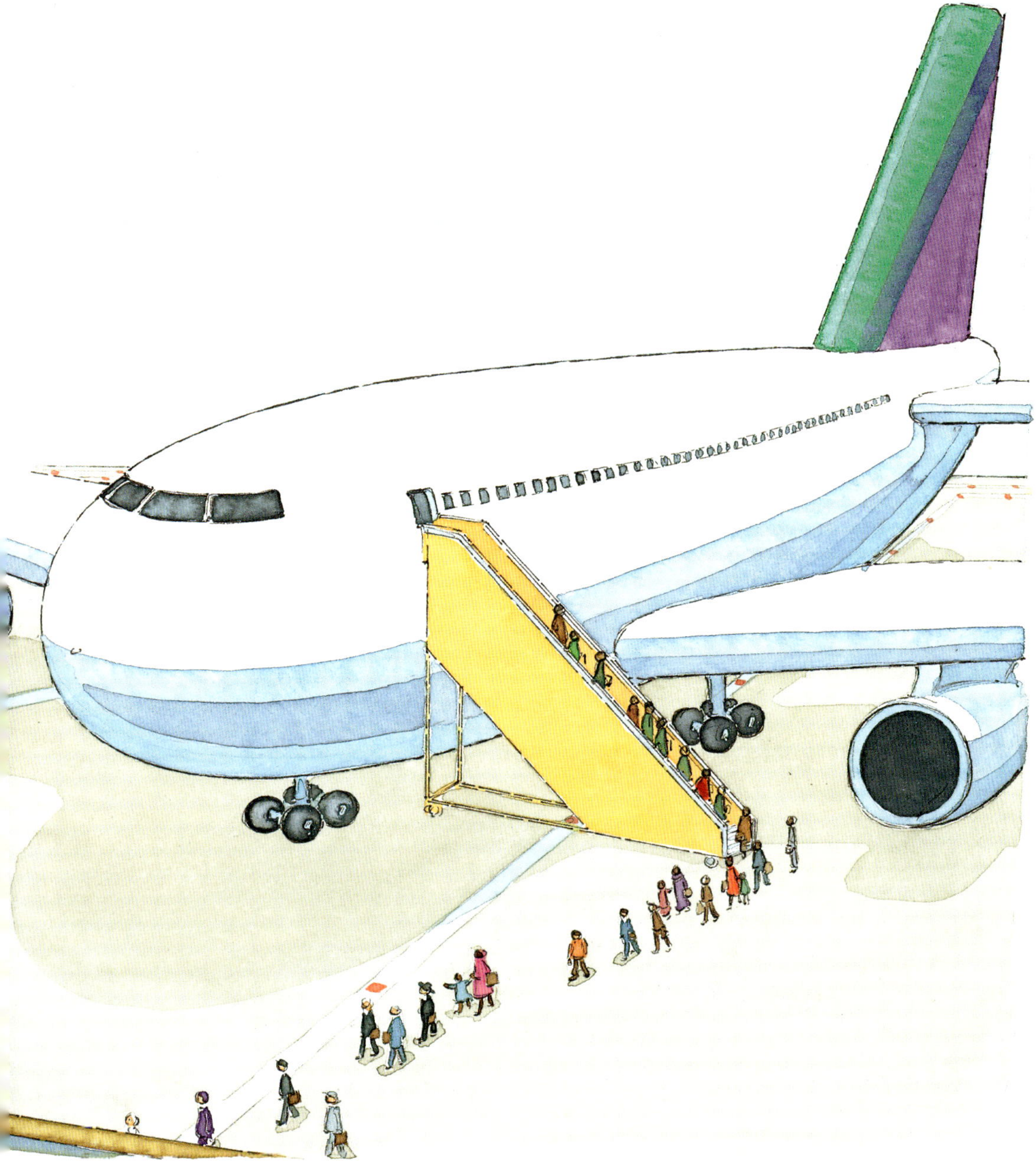

“Look, Ben,” said Mom.

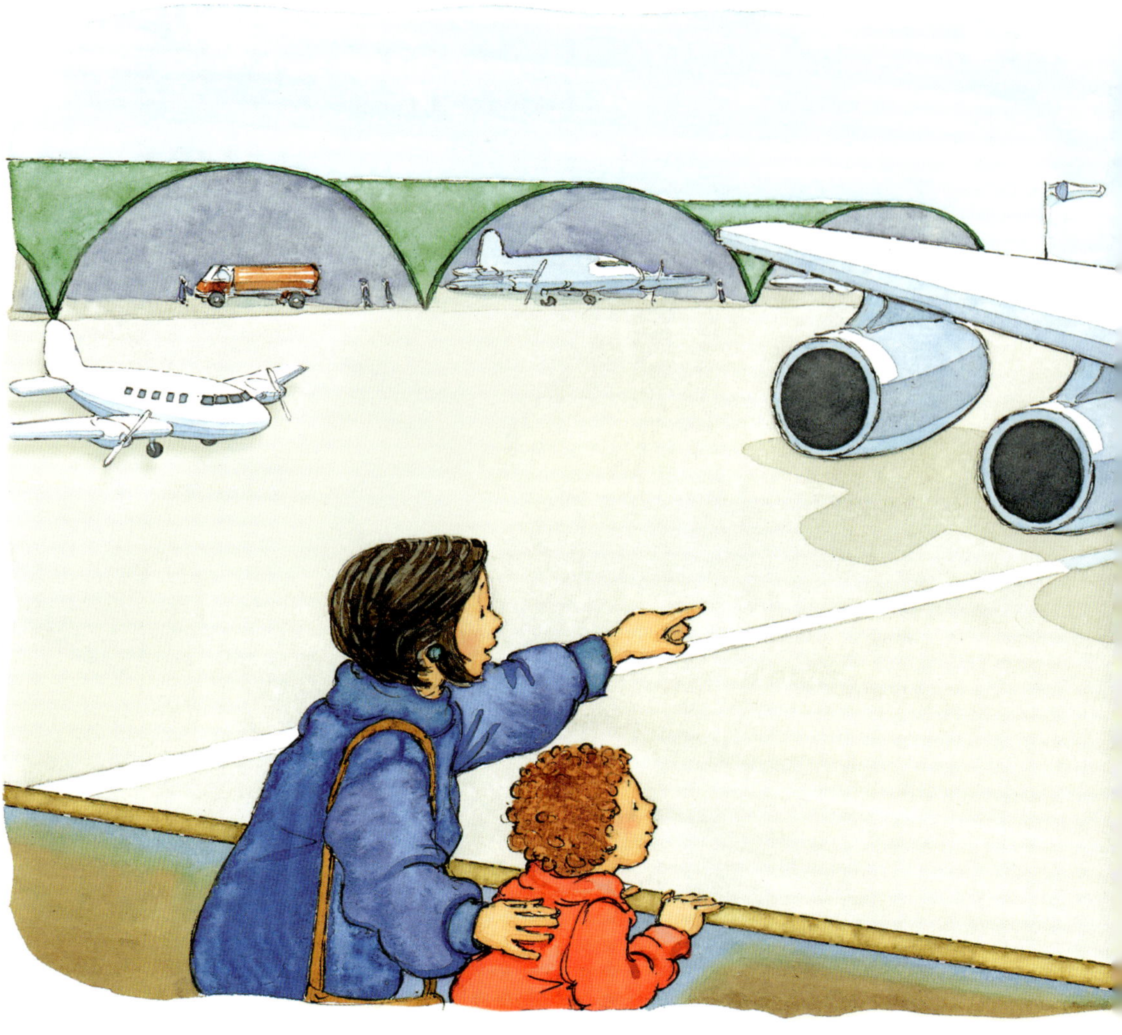

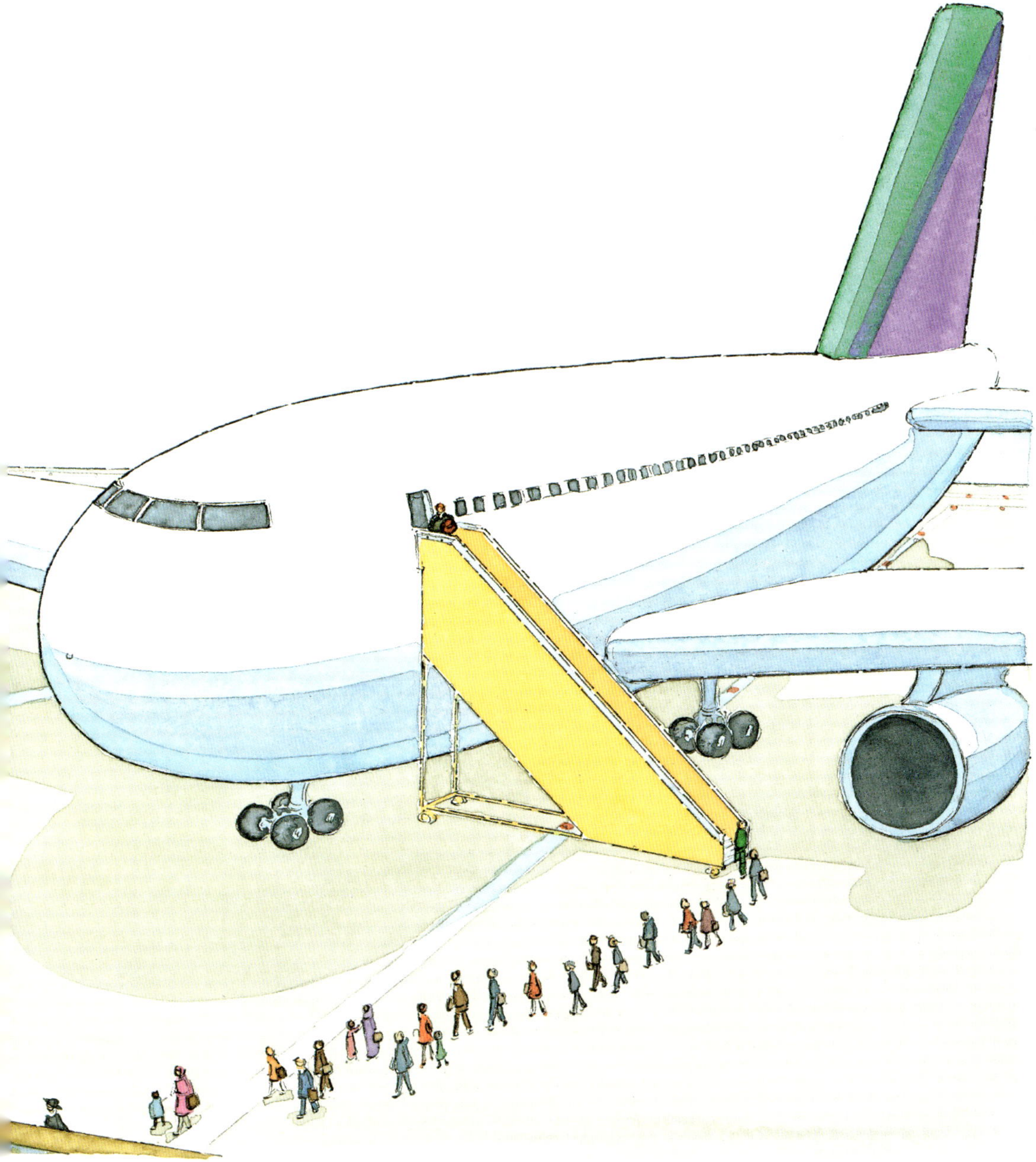

"Here comes Dad!"

shouted Ben.

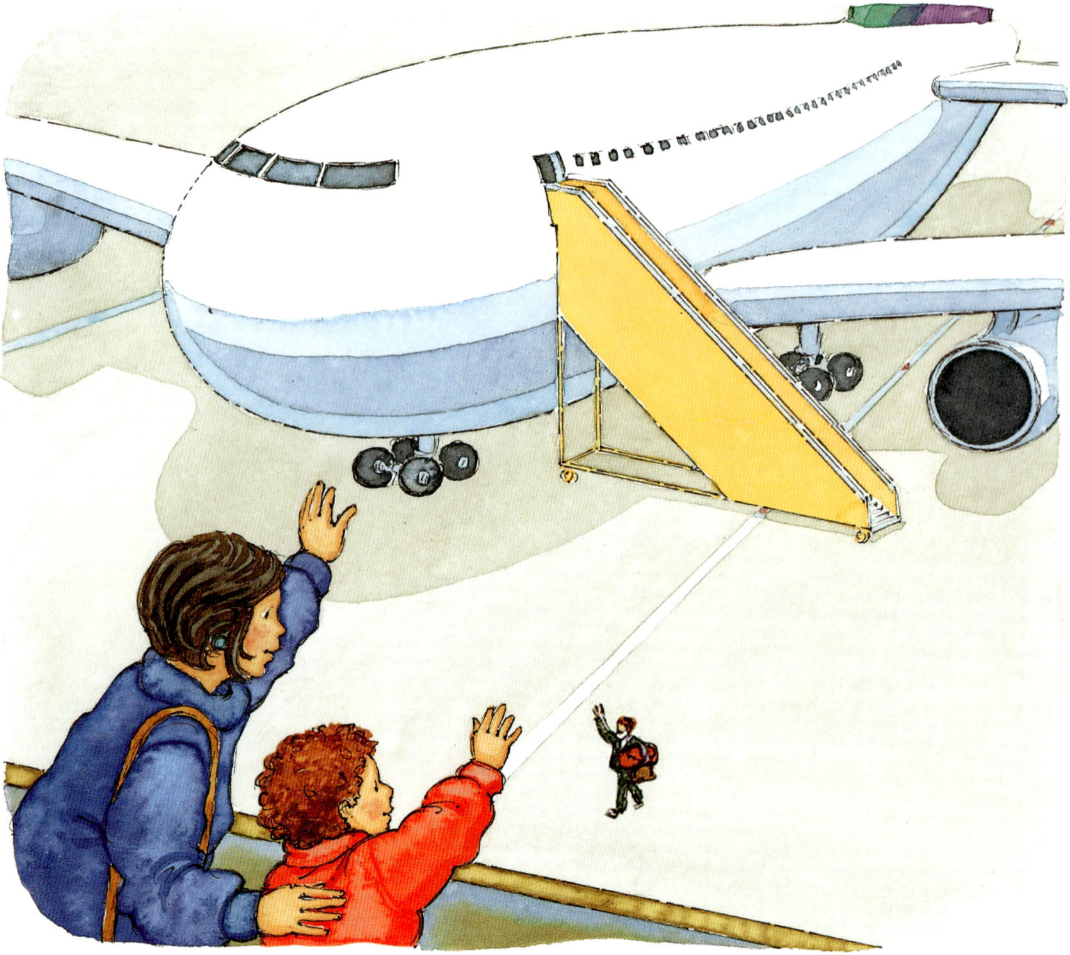